THE WEAPONS ENCYCLOPÆDIA

TANK AIRCRAFT AFV SHIP ARTILLERY VEHICLES SECRET WEAPON

TWE-003 EN

ITALIAN SELF-PROPELLED 75-18 AND 75-34

THE WEAPONS ENCYCLOPAEDIA

PUBLISHED BY

Luca Cristini Editore (Soldiershop), via Orio, 35/4 - 24050 Zanica (BG) ITALY.

DISTRIBUTION BY

Soldiershop - www.soldiershop.com, Amazon, Ingram Spark, Berliner Zinnfigurem (D), LaFeltrinelli, Mondadori, Libera Editorial (Spain), Google book (eBook), Kobo, (eBoook), Apple Book (eBook).

PUBLISHING'S NOTES

None of unpublished images or text of our book may be reproduced in any format without the expressed written permission of Luca Cristini Editore (already Soldiershop.com) when not indicate as marked with license creative commons 3.0 or 4.0. Luca Cristini Editore has made every reasonable effort to locate, contact and acknowledge rights holders and to correctly apply terms and conditions to Content. Every effort has been made to trace the copyright of all the photographs. If there are unintentional omissions, please contact the publisher in writing at: info@soldiershop.com, who will correct all subsequent editions.

LICENSES COMMONS

This book may utilize part of material marked with license creative commons 3.0 or 4.0 (CC BY 4.0), (CC BY-ND 4.0), (CC BY-SA 4.0) or (CC0 1.0). We give appropriate attribution credit and indicate if change were made in the acknowledgments field. Our WTW books series utilize only fonts licensed under the SIL Open Font License or other free use license.

CONTRIBUTORS OF THIS VOLUME & ACKNOWLEDGEMENTS

We thank the main contributors to this issue: The profiles of the tanks are all by the author. Photo coloring by Anna Cristini. Special thanks to national and/or private institutions such as: Army General Staff, State Archives, Bundesarchiv, Nara, Library of Congress, etc. To P. Crippa, A.Lopez, L.Manes, C.Cucut, Tallillo archives, for making available images or other of their archives. Special thanks to "Minstrel" who edited the corrections of the English text.

For a complete list of Soldiershop titles, or for every information please contact us on our website: www.soldiershop.com or www. cristinieditore.com. E-mail: info@soldiershop.com. Keep up to date on Facebook & Twitter: https://www.facebook.com/soldiershop. publishing

Title: **ITALIAN "SEMOVENTE" 75/18 AND 75/34** Code.: **TWE-003 EN**
Series edited by L. S. Cristini.
ISBN code: 978-88-9328829. First edition: settembre 2022
THE WEAPONS ENCYCLOPAEDIA (SOLDIERSHOP) trademark of Luca Cristini Editore.

THE WEAPONS ENCYCLOPÆDIA

TANK AIRCRAFT AFV SHIP ARTILLERY VEHICLES SECRET WEAPON

ITALIAN "SEMOVENTE" 75/18 AND 75/34

LUCA STEFANO CRISTINI

BOOK SERIES FOR MODELERS & COLLECTORS

CONTENTS

▼ Self-propelled 75/18 M.41 parade through *Via dei Fori Imperiali* in Rome. State Archives. Author's coloring.

INTRODUCTION

The self-propelled 75/18 belonged to the family of Italian assault guns, designed precisely to support medium tanks that, alone, could not counter enemy armour. The vehicles were all based on the medium tank chassis in its different variants: the M13/40, M14/41 and M15/42. The first version, the best known, was armed with an Ansaldo 75 mm L/18 cannon placed in the casemate. The 75/18 and its later version, 75/34, with a longer barrel were, during World War II, able to fight on equal terms against almost all opposing armored vehicles. As evidence of the basic quality of the vehicle, it should be mentioned that even the Wehrmacht, usually not very complementary in its "unofficial" judgments of Italian vehicles, found instead the Sermovente very well made, so much so that after September 8 it was the Italian vehicle it used the most. As mentioned, its versatility allowed the *Royal Army* its use in various roles, but especially in the support of the infantry, against enemy armour aeither on its own or supporting Italian tanks in action. A total of 225 to 360 vehicles were produced among the various versions. The progress of the war meant that Italy needed to produce versatile and well armed vehicles to counter their enemies in the field particularly the British in the Western Desert and later the Russians when Italy supported the Germans invasion. The Sermovente whilst not without its flaws gave good service to all who used them , an equivalent to the Sturmgeshutz of the German army and applied in a similar way.

■ THE DEVELOPMENT

The planning for the new weapon began in Ansaldo-Fossati in 1938, the year after the M40 medium tank was launched. The designer was Giuseppe Rosini. Initially, a 47mm cannon was planned, but military experience soon brought about a change of mind and the choice fell on the more powerful 75/18 Mod. 1934 howitzer, already known as an excellent artillery piece. It was decided to take advantage of the hull of the M40 medium tanks, and then the later M41 and M42. The choice of the 75 mm caliber was also suggested by the tactical experience learned by German tanks equipped with a similar gun. The father of the weapon choice was Sergio Berlese, a colonel in the *Artillery Technical Service* (STA or Servizio Tecnico Artiglieria), who worked in collaboration with Ansaldo engineers. As early as mid-1941, after witnessing the effectiveness of the vehicle in comparative tests, the self-propelled vehicle was immediately ordered

▼ M40 self-propelled tank with 75/18 cannon in the Ansaldo factory in Genoa. This is one of the first examples produced by the Ligurian company. State Archives.

and put into production. Nevertheless, the first vehicles did not reach North Africa until 1942. Moreover, despite its good results, the vehicle was not produced in sufficient numbers, due to an archaic idea within the General Staff that considered "double" artillery, albeit mechanized, to be almost useless. By the time it was seen that the 75/18 was the only vehicle, or close to it, that could counter the opponent's vehicles, it was too late, with the rgearing up to mass production of the assembly lines only occurring in 1943, by which time Italy was fated to experience major events leading to the downfall of the Fascist regime.

As mentioned, the vehicle, beyond the armament and its rigid casemate arrangement, had the same technical characteristics as its parent vehicle, the M tank. The crew in this case was reduced to three men: the driver, as in the M tank, was positioned in front, on the left side, with the loader behind him; the tank commander sat on the right side and had to take care of aiming and firing the gun as well as giving orders to the crew; finally, the loader also acted as a radio marcher/operator.

ARMAMENT OF THE SELF-PROPELLED GUN

The main armament, initially, was the 75/18 gun. There were also proposals to upgun the Semovente with the 75/34 piece, but this remained in the planning stage until 1942/43, (when it too saw the light of day). The gun was centrally located at the front of the casemate and housed on a pivoting ball mount, which allowed the gun a good angle of movement both vertically and horizontally, providing at least some compensation for the lack of a movable turret. The 75/18 was a fairly modern artillery piece and had long been supplied to the army in its field version. In the case of the self-propelled gun, it was equipped, at the apex, with a muzzle brake with small burst holes. The normal ammunition complement carried inside each vehicle was 41 rounds. Although this cannon had a low initial speed, it had a range of 9 km in the artillery version and slightly less mounted in the Sermovente. Once deployed, the 75/18 soon proved to

▲ The 75/18 mod. 35 howitzer, shown here in the artillery version, was a truly worthy and modern piece. Saumur Museum (France).

▲ Various details of the 75/18 M14/41 self-propelled gun on display at the Militaria exhibition in Novegro. On the left you can see the breech, the driver's seats and the interesting shape of the 'cartridge box' located below the gun; on the right the lubrication tanks and control systems of the self-propelled vehicle. Photo by the author.

▲ Other details of the self-propelled 75/18 M14/41 exhibited at the Militaria fair in Novegro (MI) in 2022. On the left you can see the radio apparatus and a tank driver's helmet; on the right the driver's seat. Photo by the author.

▲ Picture of the cannon breech inside the casemate. Photo by the author (Militaria Novegro 2022).

be a highly effective weapon that claimed many victims including tanks like the American M3 Grants, M4 Sherman or the British Mk Vlll Cromwell. The 75/18 self-propelled gun also acted as mobile artillery, providing indirect supporting fire to the assaulting infantry battalions. For secondary armament, like the medium tanks, the Sermovente also had a Breda Mod. 38 machine gun. This could also be used as an anti-aircraft gun and to avoid complications caused by smoke filling the casemate inside the self-propelled vehicle after a few shots were fired, it was usual to leave the hatches open on the top of the vehicle.

PRODUCTION

The first prototype of the self-propelled 75/18 saw the light of day in February 1941. It was mounted on the M40 hull and 30 examples were immediately ordered. On 30 April, the first vehicles were delivered to the 133rd Armoured Division 'Littorio' and the 133rd Artillery Regiment. Each delivery group consisted of two batteries of four self-propelled vehicles for a total of eight self-propelled guns, four command-tanks and a reserve of two self-propelled vehicles and one command-tank. A few months later, at the beginning of 1942, the vehicles were embarked for the African theatre and here reassigned to the 132nd Regiment of the 132nd Armoured Division 'Ariete', which was located in El-Agheila. In Libya, the self-propelled vehicles had their baptism of fire in the spring of 1942 and remained active throughout until the defeat suffered at El Alamein in November of the same year. From the first battles in the desert against enemy forces, it was realised that the guns had an inadequate amount of ammunition on board. To make up for this, the self-propelled vehicles were accompanied by Saharan trucks adapted to transport extra ammunition for the 75/18, while suitable trailers such as the Camion Bianchi, the Lancia Ro or the Rimorchio Viberti were used for transport over long distances. In June 1942, it was decided to upgrade to the new improved M14/41 hull.

This new production went on to supply the divisions of the 'Littorio', 'Ariete' and the 131st Armoured Division 'Centauro'. Numbered DLI to DLXI, all operational and deployed in Libya and Tunisia, due to adverse fortunes, they ended up being destroyed for the most part despite achieving some successes. Only those remaining in Italy were saved, the rest being captured with the fall of Tunisia. Subsequently, the third version, based on the M15/42 hull, was built and went to equip the new divisions, including the 'Lancieri di Vittorio Emanuele II' Regiment of the reborn 'Ariete' Division. The 75/18 was later joined by the very last 75/34 self-propelled vehicles. Another tank battalion equipped with the new M42s was assigned to the 12th Infantry Division 'Sassari', which flanked the armoured division 'Ariete' on 9 September in an attempt to bar the Germans' way to Rome. After the armistice, most, if not all, of these vehicles were handed over to the Germans. The only 75/18 self-propelled vehicles that remained in Italian hands were the M42s of the DLXI Group that remained in Sardinia, but due to the continued mistrust of the Allies, these vehicles remained almost non-operational.

TECHNICAL FEATURES

The tank consisted of the chassis or hull, the armament, the engine and its transmission, steering and control components. It had a mass that varied, depending on the model, between 13 and 14 tonnes. It was 4.9 to 5.06 metres long, 2.28 metres wide and 1.85 metres high including the periscope used for observation.

These are the main parts: hull - accesses - inspection hatches - exhaust holes - means of visibility - engine - transmission systems - steering and braking systems - drive and suspension.

Hull: made of special steel plates (forming the armour plating) rigidly connected on the inside by a strong framework of sections and reinforced by crossbeams, so as to obtain a watertight case resistant to the most violent stresses and shocks.

In the lower part, the hull was watertight, which allowed it to ford torrents.

▼ Interior of the combat hull. Note the black-coloured spyhole at the rear. Photo by the author (Militaria Novegro 2022)

The plates making up the armour were of different thicknesses and distributed in such a way as to ensure maximum protection for the parts most exposed to fire. Inside, the hull was divided into two parts by a vertical bulkhead to form an engine compartment at the rear and a fighting compartment at the front. The engine space contains, in addition to the engine with fans and radiators, the two fuel tanks and the accumulator batteries. The combat space comprises the middle and front parts of the hull; it contains all the tank's steering and transmission components.

The 'low' combat casemate, a good 50 mm thick, housed the crew of three men and racks for ammunition, the radio station, personal weapons, the Breda mod. 30 and its ammunition. The roof of the combat area had two hatches that opened outwards. On the top of the turret was a support for the installation of the machine gun for firing and anti-aircraft defence, while on the left side of the roof was the support for the antenna of the transceiver station and, on the right side, that for the panoramic telescope intended for the exploration of the surrounding area. The electrical system differed from that of the M tanks in that it had a single battery pack, located on the engine chamber and comprising four Magneti Marelli 3NF-12-1-24 type batteries; each had a voltage of 6 volts and were connected in series. However, the hull also incorporated some modifications, such as air filters and new silencers.

Access: a double hatch for the entire crew. The hatch on the roof, divided in two, could be kept open by means of two props.

Inspection hatches: two on the engine chamber and two for the brakes.
The two engine bonnet hatches were attached to a central hinge. They were closed from the outside by means of two bolts with wing nuts; from the inside by means of a safety catch.
The access panels for inspecting the brakes could only be opened from inside the tank by means of a device controlled by hand by the driver. This device made it possible to keep the doors partially open during travel for cooling the brakes.

▼ Interior of the hull. Visible are the seats occupied by the driver and loader, on the left of the instrument bench. Photo by the author (Militaria Novegro 2022).

Means of visibility from inside the tank: the driver had a rectangular slot cut into the front plate of the hull, with a hinged hatch on the outside and operated with a lever from the inside. The hatch could assume a fully open position -remaining almost horizontal- and all other intermediate positions until fully closed. With the hatch closed, direct visibility was possible through a longitudinal slit in the hatch, which could be closed from the inside by means of a plate fixed to the hatch and operated with a special pin. The driver's eyes were protected from splinters by a glass block contained in a box attached to the plate and easily removable.

In addition to direct visibility, the driver had at his disposal a means of indirect visibility consisting of a hyposcope. This apparatus, which allowed the tank to be guided when it was necessary to keep the driving hatch closed during combat, was essentially composed of two prisms, an upper one -objective- protruding from the roof of the hull, and a lower one -ocular- placed in the interior at the driver's eye level. For rear and lateral visibility, the tank leader and the loader faced the outside of the hull with the hatches open, no slits were provided apart from two minute circular ones protected by pivoting plates located on the sides of the rear wall. However, a periscope and other sights were available for the commander.

Engine: Four-stroke, diesel type; 8 cylinders in a block -four on each side- arranged at 90°, V-position. This type of engine differed fundamentally from the petroleum fuelled internal combustion engine found in many armoured vehicles of the time and had some advantage for the crew in case of fire. For fuelling, unlike in normal internal combustion engines, in injection engines there was no fuel to prepare the mixture of air and petrol outside the cylinder.

In this engine, the intake into the cylinder was taken directly from the atmosphere; only a filter was installed at the end of the intake duct to trap any impurities and dust in the air. At the end of suction, only air was introduced into the cylinder, on which normal pressure was then exerted during the upward stroke of the piston. The fuel for injection into the cylinders was supplied by special injection pumps, one for each cylinder, grouped together in a single mechanical unit, controlled with appropriate transmission from the engine. Ignition of the injected fuel took place by the diesel principle (except for the first cold engine start, which was facilitated by the spark plugs, powered by a current of 2 volts). After this came the normal bursting phase and then the exhaust phase, the final phase of the operating cycle, which was renewed in full, as in all normal four-stroke internal combustion engines. Starting with the M41 version, the interior of the self-propelled engine was adapted to accommodate the improved 15T injection engine to replace the 8T, which also powered the M13/40.

Engine start-up: 1) *By hand*, either from inside or outside the tank, by means of a hand-crank-operated inertia starter equipped with a starter button.

2) *Electric*, by means of two starter motors acting on a gear wheel attached to the flywheel.

Lubrication: the oil was circulated by means of three pumps in a single casing, two of which were recovery pumps and one delivery pump. The scavenge pumps drew oil from the two sumps in the engine sump and sent it to the sump.

Cooling: This was by forced water circulation using a centrifugal pump. The pump was driven by a double chain and a sprocket on the crankshaft. Water cooling was achieved by fans blowing air through the two radiators.

Air filters: there were four of them, attached to the engine, two on each side; they consisted of the inside housed a filter of special fabric. Their task was to filter the air before it entered the cylinders during the intake phase.

Transmission-clutch parts: incorporated into the engine flywheel, it consisted of: a clutch drive housing; a pressure plate ring; a friction disc on the drive shaft; twelve springs. The clutch was disengaged by actuating the pedal; this, with special tie rods and levers, controlled the clutch release sleeve, which in turn caused the pressure plate to move away by compressing the springs more.

Transmission: the drive shaft was used to transmit the movement of the crankshaft to the gearbox and planetary assembly arranged at the front of the tank. The shaft was protected by a tube and protective cap and fitted with universal joints.

Gearbox: the gearbox was of the sliding block type, with gears always engaged and direct drive. Three shafts: primary, subsidiary, secondary and a reverse gear shaft. In the box, separated by a wall, was the speed reducer, which allowed a reduction to be made to the normal gears. Therefore there were four normal and four reduced gears. A special lever was used to engage this reduction and directly connect the secondary shaft of the gearbox with the axle, i.e., the truncated cone and epicycle assembly.

Direction and braking systems: they were part of an epicycle complex which was designed to allow: a) transmission of motion to the wheels; b) direction; c) braking. To control the driving of the tank, two direction levers were arranged on the left side of the driver. Operating these levers caused the braking of the tracks and consequently the steering of the tank, which pivoted on the braked track.

Tank braking: slowing down and stopping the tank was achieved by acting simultaneously on the two direction levers; to have more vigorous braking, the brake pedal was pressed simultaneously, which therefore functioned to enhance the braking action.

External propulsion and suspension systems - Drive wheels: located on the sides of the hull at the front, they received motion from the drive shafts. These consisted of a wheel with two flanges to which two toothed rings were attached for transmitting motion to the track. Also attached to the inner flanges of the wheels were internally toothed crown wheels with pinions that received motion from the driveshafts and protruded from the front circular openings of the hull.

▲ Picture of the self-propelled 75/18 M14-41. Photo by the author (Militaria Novegro 2022).

Tracks: each track consisted of 8 links equal to each other and hinged together by means of pins, the slipping out of which was prevented, on the one hand, by a stop in the hole of the last hinge and, on the other, by a stop pad embedded in a slot in the links. In the center each link carried a guide fin and, on either side of that fin, two rectangular holes into which the teeth of the drive wheels were inserted.

Idler wheels and idler assemblies: the two tracks were supported by the drive wheels and also tensioned on two idler wheels, the pivots of which were carried by longitudinally displaceable idler arms. Movement caused the track to increase tension or loosen.

Guide rollers: each track was guided and rested its upper branch on three rubberized rollers, rotating on pins attached to the sides of the hull.

Suspension: the tank, through the pins of four plates nailed to the hull sides, rested elastically on four bogies, two on each side. The bogies, each consisting of two pairs of rubberized rollers, were located on the sides of the hull so that the load was evenly distributed on each.
Each bogie was independent of the others and had the ability to swing around the pivot of the relevant plate. The elastic system, consisting of springs, levers and rocker arms that made it up, not only ensured the elastic suspension of the tank, but also allowed the undercarriage to deform so that the track could adapt to any roughness in the terrain and keep in constant contact with the rollers of the undercarriage. With this, one of the main causes of skidding was eliminated.

Armor: the type of construction and materials used in Italian tanks were not up to the standard of foreign production, especially with regard to the chemical composition of the armor plates.
The armor was also bolted on (an Italian characteristic in WW2 armored vehicles), and not cast. The armor often tended to split on impact with an enemy projectile, even if there was no penetration, because it was too "rigid," not very malleable, and poorly treated. The armor reached a maximum of 50mm at the front of the casemate and a minimum of 14mm at the bottom of the hull.

Internal arrangement: engine starting was either electrically or by hand by means of an inertia starter, which could be operated either outside or inside the vehicle.
The tank was equipped with an electrical system that provided external lighting hull and a single light placed in the rear) and internal lighting with two bulbs on the dashboard and two in the fighting chamber. The system, of course, also provided engine starting.
Elevation, and gun arc, were controlled by hand by means of two hand wheels to the left of the gunner/leader. All optical instruments on board were built by the St. George company.

Radio system: the radio system, which was almost completely absent in the first tanks produced, consisted of a set of the type "RF1 CA" , located on the right side of the hull.
A telegraph was not mounted for internal communications, as in the case of M tanks, since, lacking the turret, the three men were all at the same height and in a cramped space were in direct communication.

Source: S.M.R.E. - *"Notions of weapons, firing and various materials"*, Edizioni Le "Forze Armate,"
Rome, 1942.

Endnotes

British technicians from the Cobham School of Tank Technology examined a self-propelled 75/18 M40 captured in Africa and wrote a flattering report, although it did not mention the effectiveness of the armament. In objective terms, the British praised the mechanics, calling it efficient and practical, especially the suspension and steering. The 8T engine, while underpowered, was considered very compact and easily accessible. The only criticisms were made of the armor, according to them, still below acceptable standards for the Allies, and both the absence of splinter protection and the exposure of the suspension, which was particularly vulnerable to anti-tank mines, were complained about.

SELF-PROPELLED 75/18 M13-40 PROTOTYPE, GENOA, ITALY 1941

▲ Prototype of the self-propelled 75/18 M.40 in the Ansaldo factory in Genoa, Italy 1941.

VERSIONS OF THE VEHICLES

As was the case with medium tanks, also in the case of self-propelled vehicles, three main versions were made from their derivatives for the Royal Army, including definitive operatives and prototypes. The most important ones are set out below.

- *75/18 M13/40*: first designation of the self-propelled vehicle, designed by Ansaldo in 1938. This first version was produced in only 60 units, in two production runs. The armament was based mainly on the 75/18 mod. 1935 cannon and Breda mod. 30 machine gun aboard the vehicle. The M13/40 was powered by a liquid-cooled, 8-cylinder SPA 8T diesel engine. The associated speed gearbox had 4 forward gears and a normal reverse gear; in addition, thanks to the built-in gearbox, there were 4 more reduction gears plus an additional reverse gear. The engine chosen was one of the tank's major handicaps: low powered and subject to various failures, due to sand and because of the deplorable lack of filters. It weighed 13 tons, had a maximum speed of 33 km/h and a range of 215 km.

- *75/18 M14/41*: the successor model to the first was produced in 162 units (some sources claim 300 units) and equipped with the new 145 hp Fiat SPA 15T V-8 diesel engine. The vehicle was almost identical to its predecessor, both in mechanics and armament. The hull differed only in the shape of the extended track covers along the entire length of the tank and other small details. The new engine also involved new radiator grilles, with fins oriented parallel to the tank's major axis. A mud-hunting lever for the drive wheel was introduced, as well as other improvements involving the electrical system. Also identical was the armament and its arrangement. In addition to the combat vehicles, several radio command tanks were also produced. It weighed 13.5 tons, so it was somewhat heavier than its predecessor. Thanks to the new engine it enjoyed a slightly higher speed (35 km/h).

- *75/18 M15/42*: produced in an uncertain but rather low number, it was the third and final general improvement in every respect, but considering the times, it came too late to be able to face the new enemy

▲ Self-propelled version on M.13-40 hull (recognisable by the partial wing). Saumur Museum, Wikipedia.

tanks on a par. Due to the consequent events of the Cassibile armistice of September 3, production was soon discontinued. The last model in the series was delivered in May 1943. The number of units delivered to the Royal Army was, as mentioned, only 60, while the others ended up being used by the Germans (who put it back into production) and the regular army of the Italian Social Republic. The main differences with the earlier versions were: a longer length of the vehicle at the rear of about 15cm; the placement of the spare wheels on the bottom of the tank. After September 8, 1943, as mentioned, the Germans took possession of all Italian self-propelled vehicles (excluding those located in Sardinia). They then ordered new production of 75/18 and 75/34, which were delivered in 1944. The weight was now 15 tons, with improved protection, and a length increased by about six inches. Speed, thanks to a third new engine, was now 39 km(h). It also had smoke grenade launchers carried in a box at the rear of the hull.

The tanks used by the Germans were renamed *StuG M42 mit 75/34* (851), all regularly equipped with an RF1 CA radio and immediately distributed to armored detachments in the Germanic Army.

DERIVATIVES OF SELF-PROPELLED 75/18

- *75/34 M15/42:* another version of the self-propelled gun was the 75/34 on an M.42 hull, preceded by a prototype armed with a 75/32 Mod. 1937 that did not pass trials. The improved, and later produced, version enjoyed a 75/34 Mod. SF gun equipped with a longer barrel and more powerful ammunition, which greatly increased anti-tank performance. Ordered in as many as 253 units, only sixty were produced and delivered to large armored units in August 1943. The new gun had a range up to 12,000 meters. The forward speed also underwent a significant increase.

- *M.40, M.41 and M.42 command tanks:* along with the 75/18 self-propelled gun, by order of the General Staff, the related command tank variant was developed. It was basically a normal medium tank

▲ Two pictures of the self-propelled 75/34 M.15-42 with the new, longer and more powerful barrel (State Archives).

▲ Column of 75/18 self-propelled vehicles in southern Italy around 1942. Note in the front row a command vehicle with two twin machine guns derived from the M40 medium tank. State Archives. Author's colouring.

without a turret and equipped with the necessary equipment for battery firing direction and radio links. The turret compartment, initially enclosed, had an upper access with the same two hatches as the original tank. During series production, however, a total of four hatches were cut out, allowing more space for observers. The combat space housed the four-person crew: the driver on the left and the gunner on the right; on the two rear seats took their places the commander and the signaller. The gunner was in charge of the two 8-mm Breda 38s on the M40, which were replaced by a single 13.2-mm Breda Mod. 31 in later versions; another 8-mm Breda machine gun with a special wolf's mouth mount for antiaircraft fire was also located in the compartment. Finally, inside the vehicle were distributed ammunition, optical equipment, control instruments, and steering gear. On the upper and rear ends of the right side of the roof were the mounts for the two radio transmitter station antennas. The panoramic telescope was placed on the left corner of the roof. Produced in a total of 139 units, they served mainly to direct the fire of artillery self-propelled vehicles. Two Magneti Marelli radios, one RF1 CA and one RF2 CA, and two extra batteries were placed in the casemate; finally, a rangefinder was installed.
A curiosity: a signal gun with 45 rounds was stored inside the vehicle. Each battery consisted of eight self-propelled guns and two command tanks.

- *M14/41 Radio Tank:* in addition to the standard Magneti Marelli RF1 CA radio, it was equipped with an RF2 CA. The antennas were mounted on the left side of the hull and, by means of a knob, it was possible to lower them from inside the combat chamber to allow rotation of the turret to that side. This craft, if intended for airborne communication, was eventually also equipped with the RF3M radio. This had a longer signal range than the RF2CA radio device. Thirty-four units of the M14/41CR were produced, which were distributed at the rate of two vehicles per battalion command.

▲ M14-41 Command Tank. In the small photo the march of the self-propelled tanks in the Libyan desert. (Archive P. Crippa. Author's colouring)

SELF-PROPELLED 75/18 M14-41 RADIO CONTROL TANK IN NORTH AFRICA, 1942

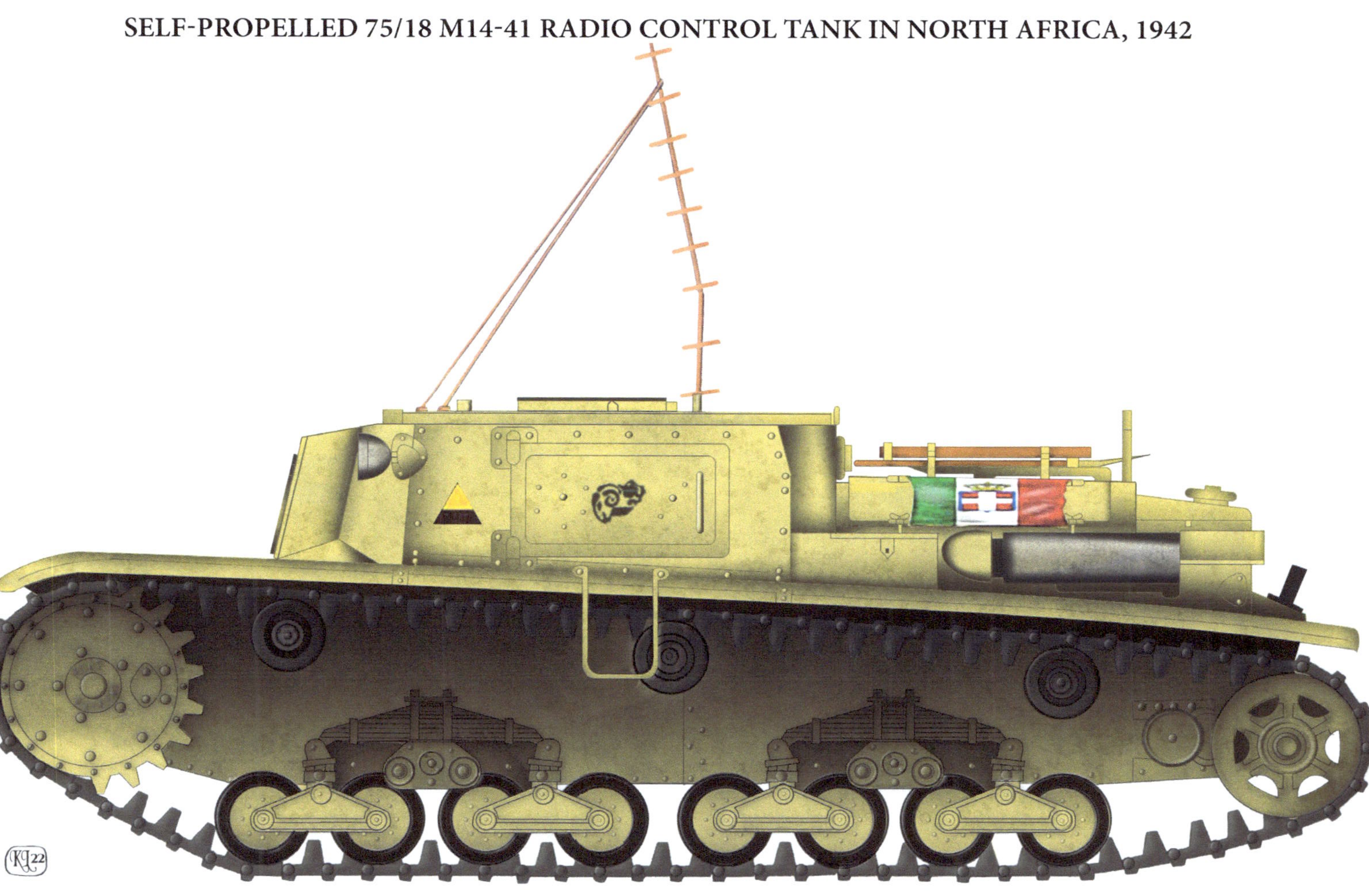

▲ Self-propelled Radio Command Tank 75/18 M.41 of the Ariete Armoured Division just landed in Libya, 1942.

▲ After the armistice of 8 September 1943, (in the small photo, a self-propelled vehicle in the Porta San Paolo area), which was conducted in a very slipshod way by the Italian General Staff, the Germans, with their usual organisation and timeliness, quickly put the disbanded Italian army out of action and seized and reused much of the war material that had already belonged to the Royal Army. In the photo you can see a considerable amount of vehicles, mainly medium tanks and self-propelled vehicles in German hands. (Archive P. Crippa. Author's colouring).

SELF-PROPELLED 75/18 M13-40, AFRICA CAMPAIGN, 1942

▲ Self-propelled 75-18 on M.40 hull. Belonging to the 5th self-propelled group, of the 132nd artillery regiment of the Ariete Armoured Division, at El Alamein, Egypt, August 1942. Note the Breda mod. 30 on the roof of the vehicle at the disposal of the tank leader.

▲ A self-propelled 75/18 hit and knocked out by British armour in the African desert. (Wikipedia, author's colouring). In the small photo a broken-down self-propelled vehicle is being towed for repairs.

ITALIAN SELF-PROPELLED 75-18 AND 75-34

OPERATIONAL DEPLOYMENT

As soon as the first 75/18 self-propelled vehicles were produced, they were delivered to the Armored Divisions primarily as divisional mobile artillery units. Only in the field did it become clear, however, that their most decisive use would be in combat against enemy tanks as the, medium tanks being at the time were ill-suited to stop opposing armored vehicles, such as the British Matilda and Crusader, but later also U.S. tanks such as the M3 Lee/Grant and M4 Sherman. The self-propelled vehicles were distributed in two groups for each armored division, which in turn consisted of 2 batteries of four self-propelled 75/18 each, four command tanks for each artillery group, and two more self-propelled vehicles and a reserve command tank, for a total of 18 self-propelled vehicles and 9 command tanks. Production of the M40 version consisted of only 60 vehicles divided into 6 groups indicated by Roman numerals from DLI to DLVI.

BAPTISM OF FIRE IN NORTHERN AFRICA

The two groups formed in 1941 carried out their training in Italy in two phases: the first concerning the use of artillery and the second the use of the armored vehicle, and were then sent into combat in North Africa. The best experience, however, was the war in the desert, where despite the known defects of the Royal Army, the use of the self-propelled vehicles was remarkably successful, especially during the second Italian-German offensive, which began from El-Agheila in January 1942, after which there was a reorganization of the units according to the new requirements. The first two batteries delivered were IV and VI, (Group DLI) and were assigned to the *"Ariete"* (132nd Armored Division) on May 14, 1942. These first two were later joined by Group DLII, also in the same division. Later a new group, DLIV, was ready, which went to arm the *131st Armored Division "Centaur"*. Finally the two groups DLV and DLVI, went to the *133rd Armored Division "Littorio"*. All personnel in the crews of the self-propelled vehicles were from artillery and not tank crews as on the M tanks.

The operational life of the 75/18 self-propelled vehicles began towards the last months of 1941, lasting

▼ Self-propelled tanks in the Libyan desert in 1942, from *Cronache di Guerra* magazine (author's collection).

until the end of the war. The most intense employment was certainly in North Africa in the ranks of the three Italian armored divisions "Ariete," "Littorio," and "Centauro," until the surrender in Tunisia in May 1943. But already at El Alamein most of the DLI, DLII, DLIV and DLVI groups were all but destroyed.

However, as mentioned, prior to El Alamein, the General Staff of the Italian forces in Libya was very complimentary about the use of armored artillery: "The self-propelled 75/18 gave excellent proof of itself, combining the power of the single shot, better technical requirements and better maneuverability than the M tank." As a result, the War Ministry decided to place an order for 163 new units of the M42 version, but they entered service too late, in May 1943.

The swan song of the self-propelled units occurred at El Alamein, the oft-mentioned Great Desert Battle. Here two armored groups of self-propelled vehicles, the DLIV and DLVI, were engaged, totaling 35 vehicles. For the occasion they were equipped with more than double the amount of rounds, over a hundred rounds per self-propelled unit. Placed around high ground numbers 33 and 34, they almost all perished except for two that managed to return. Twelve other vehicles belonging to the DLI and DLII groups, also of the "Ariete," placed in the rear of the rearguard with respect to the front line, tried in every way to stem the rushing British advance, inflicting considerable losses on the enemy (30 enemy tanks including Sherman, Grant and Crusader were reported by Italian sources). In contrast, the "Ariete" was totally destroyed. The two survivors mentioned were also lost a short time later in the defense of the Capuzzo Redoubt also in Libya.

In early 1943 the Italians managed to organize the new "Centaur" division sent to Africa from Greece. This division made up of veterans was also the only one that succeeded against the North American forces in Africa. Their greatest success, in fact, was the Battle of Kasserine in February 1943.

ITALY, SICILY

After the loss of Africa, the few self-propelled vehicles that could be saved, along with those stationed on the peninsula, were formed into the following armored units: *the 135th Armored Division "Ariete II"*,

▼ Line of self-propelled vehicles deployed in the Cyrenaean desert 1941. State Archives (author's colouring).

SELF-PROPELLED COMMAND TANK 75/18 M13-40, AFRICA CAMPAIGN, 1942.

▲ Self-propelled Command Tank 75-18 on M.40. Belonged to the Ariete Armoured Division, in Cyrenaica, February 1942.

▲ Semovente 75/18 M.41 knocked out of action in the clashes in Rome in September 1943. Bundesarchiv (author's colouring).

SELF-PROPELLED 75/18 M13-40 ON 3RO LANCIA TRUCK IN NORTH AFRICA, 1942

▲ Semovente 75/18 M.40 2nd Battery 1st Group of the Ariete Armoured Division, on Lancia 3Ro transport. Cyrenaica Desert, Libya, June 1942.

which counted among its ranks 94 M41 from 75/18 (divided between the *Reconnaissance Regiment* and the *Armored Regiments*). Other self-propelled vehicles were employed by the *Armored Motorized Regiment* stationed in Sardinia, which in fact took no part in any combat during World War II, and whose vehicles would be the only ones not to end up in German hands after the armistice.

Other self-propelled vehicles were combined with the *XII Anti-tank Group* of the *"Sassari" Infantry Division* and in the six squadrons belonging to the *"Lancieri di Vittorio Emanuele II"* Regiment.

Their first commitment was the defense of Sicily following the Allied landings in July 1943. After the loss of Sicily, Italy decisively secured its exit from the conflict by agreeing to sign, in Sicily itself, the Cassibile Accords. Then, until the armistice of September 8, and before the tragic events of the defense of Rome, the self-propelled 75/18 had no particular war commitments to report.

ITALY, ROME, SEPTEMBER 1943

From September 8 to 10, "Aries II" was involved in clashes against the Germans around and inside Rome, particularly at Porta San Paolo. There were also clashes in the town of Cesano, and on the Via Ostiense leading to Rome. But as a result of the poor or no preparation for the defense of the capital, even with more men and means, it ended up that most of the Italian troops withdrew, by superior order, to Tivoli, effectively abandoning the defense of the city. Most of the Royal Army's vehicles fell into German hands and went to equip the *2nd Fallschirmjäger-Division*.

The only noteworthy reaction on the Italian side occurred in the facts at Porta San Paolo, one of the main entrances to the city of Rome, on Sept. 10. Here, Italian soldiers of the *21st Infantry Division Grenadiers of Sardinia*, the *I Squadron* of the *'Genova Cavalry'*, some units of the *Infantry Division 'Sassari'*, Paratroopers of the *10th Arditi Parachutisti Regiment* supported by several civilians, including many women, fought heroically and with commitment against the German forces that wanted to enter the city.

On that occasion, numerous were the self-propelled 75/18s that took part in the action, as indeed testified by many photos, also published in this book.

▼ An M40 self-propelled vehicle boards on a Viberti trailer to be transported to the operational area. Note the Breda machine gun mounted on the roof of the vehicle. State Archives. Author's colouring.

▲ Self-propelled 75/18 M.41 1st Company, 31st Tank Regiment, 134th Centaur Armoured Division - El Guettar, Tunisia, January 1943.

More precisely, it was a dozen 75/18 self-propelled M41 and M42 of the *4th Tank Regiment* of the *8th Bersaglieri Brigade* commanded by Second Lieutenant Vincenzo Fioritto, who counterattacked as far as they could the German opponents of the *2nd Division Fallschirmjäger*. Fioritto himself, by the end of the day, was a casualty of the fighting. The resistance, which began at dawn on the 10th, did not end until after 5 p.m., when the remaining Italian forces retreated, later joining the Partisan forces, first making sure to put their vehicles out of action to prevent the Germans from repurposing them.

SELF-PROPELLED VEHICLES PASS TO GERMANS AND THE ITALIAN SOCIAL REPUBLIC

After the Italian surrender in September 1943, the occupying German forces used most of the captured vehicles, and among them, self-propelled vehicles were the favorite, so that production of the 75/18 also resumed with slight modifications. A second escort roll for smoke mortars was added to the back of the superstructure and the rear of the hull. The new 75/18 and 75/34, together with almost all Ansaldo production vehicles, participated from then on under the German insignia in all the battles of the Italian campaign until May 2, 1945.

In general, therefore, self-propelled vehicles also shared the fate of all Italian war materiel that the Germans found useful to redeploy. The 75/18 self-propelled vehicles were repainted with the typical German armored vehicle colors and were aggregated with their fighting units.

Some units were later granted for use to some units of the National Republican Army of the CSR. Among these, those receiving self-propelled vehicles were: the "San Giusto" Armored Squadron Group to which, in addition to four M tanks, three 75/18 self-propelled vehicles on M42 hulls and one 75/34 self-propelled vehicle on M42 hulls were also made available. The Anti-Partisan Regiment (RAP) - Exploring Group integrated two 75/18 self-propelled units on M42 hulls, while the "Leonessa" Armored Group deployed two command tanks on M42 hulls for its self-propelled battery.

The German units that most recycled captured self-propelled vehicles were: those taken in Lazio, which

▼ The same vehicle on page 28 loaded on a Viberti trailer. Note the yellow black triangle sign, typical of self-propelled vehicles in Africa. State Archives. Author's colouring.

SELF-PROPELLED COMMAND TANK 75/18 M14-41, SICILY 1943, THEN IN TUNISIA 1943

▲ Self-propelled tank 75/18 M.41 of the 'Piscicelli' Group, Tunisia, March 1943, already in the forces of the DLVII Group operating in Sicily in January 1943. Self-propelled vehicles in the period were named after old artillery and rifles of the past.

▲ Uniform of Italian tank drivers 1940-1943, plates and symbols used on tanks and self-propelled vehicles. Artwork by the author.

ended up with the *2ⁿᵈ Fallschirmjäger Division*. All other vehicles available in German-occupied Italian territory, or captured in Albania and the Balkans, were placed on a role with the German armored divisions. Again, many (but not all) vehicles were repainted and fitted with German insignia.

Numerically, the Wehrmacht redeployed about 80 newly produced self-propelled vehicles and 36 war prey captured from the Italians, renaming the vehicle *StuG M42 mit 75/34 (851)*.

"PARTISAN" SELF-PROPELLED VEHICLES

The story of the armored vehicles that ended up in the hands of partisan forces turns out to be curious and interesting. On April 18, 1945, a large general strike broke out in the factories of Turin, as many as 12,000 Fiat workers crossed their arms in protest. Being at war, they stood in defense of the factories, organizing trenches, roadblocks and rushing to arm themselves. Everything went smoothly for a few days, but after about a week the Nazi-fascist reaction loomed. The workers thought, therefore, of using the military vehicles that were being repaired in the Fiat workshops at the time. These were specifically two M.42 tanks and a self-propelled 75/18 M.42. These three vehicles proved very useful in the days to come, contributing first to the defense of the factories and then to the defense of the important railway junction of Turin Porta Nuova.

In the last days of the war with Turin effectively liberated by its workers and citizens, a parade was held to celebrate the coming end of the war. Of course, the partisans "camouflaged" their armored vehicles with their colors and insignia. Especially the names and slogans of the resistance took the lion's share. A 75/18 M42 self-propelled vehicle was used by the *7ᵗʰ Autonomous Partisan Division "Monferrato"* and arrived in Turin on April 25, 1943, for the aforementioned parade through the city center.

This vehicle was distinguished by the inscriptions on the walls of its hull: *"W LA MONFERRATO"* and *"W STALIN"*, while on the small window/spion of the driver of the vehicle was the inscription "Ali," which was nothing but the name of the commander of the partisan unit that one night captured an armored vehicle of the "Leonessa" Group without the CSR forces noticing. Even today, it is still unclear whether this story was a myth or a legend created by the partisans. it is interesting to note that the partisan brigade in question was "autonomous," that is, it was not linked to any political group, unlike the Garibaldi Partisan Brigades, which were composed of communists, and the Matteotti Partisan Brigades, which grouped mostly socialists, or those of the Action Party with a popular and moderate orientation. This means that the partisans/workers who painted *"W STALIN"* on the hull did so out of caution in order to avoid friendly fire.

Other 75/18 self-propelled vehicles used by partisans were seen in Milan, Genoa and other northern Italian cities that were liberated from Nazi-Fascist oppression in the days between April 24 and 30.

CONCLUSIONS

A total of 62 self-propelled vehicles survived the war, including 50 M41 75/18 and 12 M42 75/18, which were largely reused by the Italian Army from 1946 to November 1955. They began to be withdrawn only around 1953, when the newer and more powerful M47 Patton arrived from the United States.

In 1955 they were completely withdrawn from service, but still remained in reserve until 1965 when most of them were scrapped. 21 of them were repaired by the Turin arsenal between 1945 and 1950. Many of these self-propelled guns are now preserved in museums, civic parks or collections in Italy.

The 75/18 self-propelled gun was one of the few Italian vehicles to hold its own for some time against the opposing vehicles, although it was obviously not without serious shortcomings. Among them, the most interesting to note were: the modest amount of ammunition carried, only 44 rounds, which in fact limited its combat performance quite a bit, forcing the use and support of accessory supply vehicles, by their very nature, very vulnerable. The range and power of the 75/18 gun soon proved to be lacking in comparison with allied self-propelled guns, such as the Priest or Sexton, or the Wespe. Things improved with the new calibers of the latest self-propelled guns, but by then it was too late. Another major problem was the deficient secondary armament, totally lacking a coaxial machine gun, which made the vehicle very vulnerable to infantry attacks. Further problems, finally, stemmed from the poor nature of the M hull, its speed, critical suspension, etc.

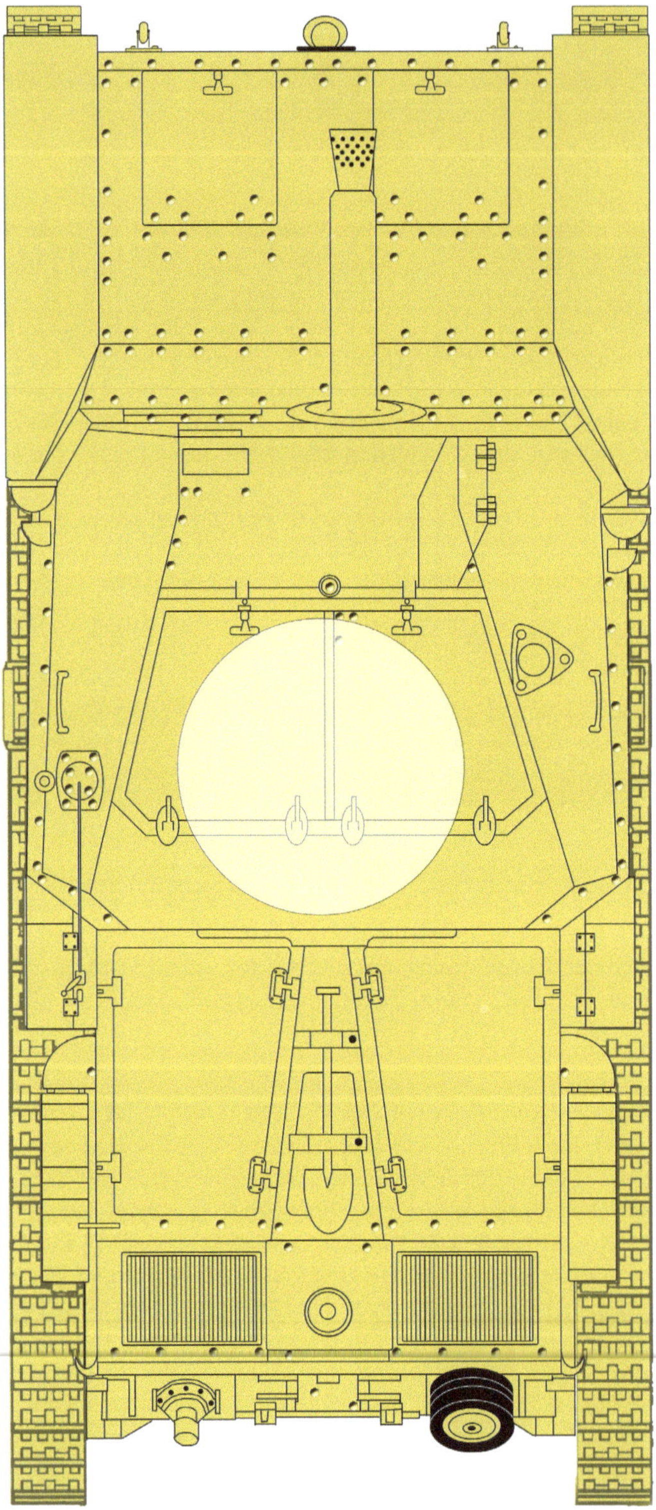

▲ View of the Italian 75/18 M.40 self-propelled aircraft from above. Clearly visible on the casemate roof is the painted white circle for air recognition by friendly aircraft. On the right, the bronze or aluminium badge was placed on the front plate of the armoured vehicles from April 1936 to August 1943.

SELF-PROPELLED 75/18 M15-42 IN ROME, SEPTEMBER 1943

▲ Self-propelled 75/18 M.42 of the "Sassari" XIII Infantry Battalion, II Company in Rome, Italy 9 September 1943.

▲ Libyan front: in the foreground a 75/18 M41 and in the background General Erwin Rommel in a military car. Bundesarchiv - author's colouring.

▼ Front view of a self-propelled vehicle in motion. Paolo Crippa Archive.

SELF-PROPELLED 75/18 M14-41 IN ROME, SEPTEMBER 1943

▲ Self-propelled 75/18 M.41 of the 4th Tank Regiment at Porta San Paolo, Rome, Italy 10 September 1943.

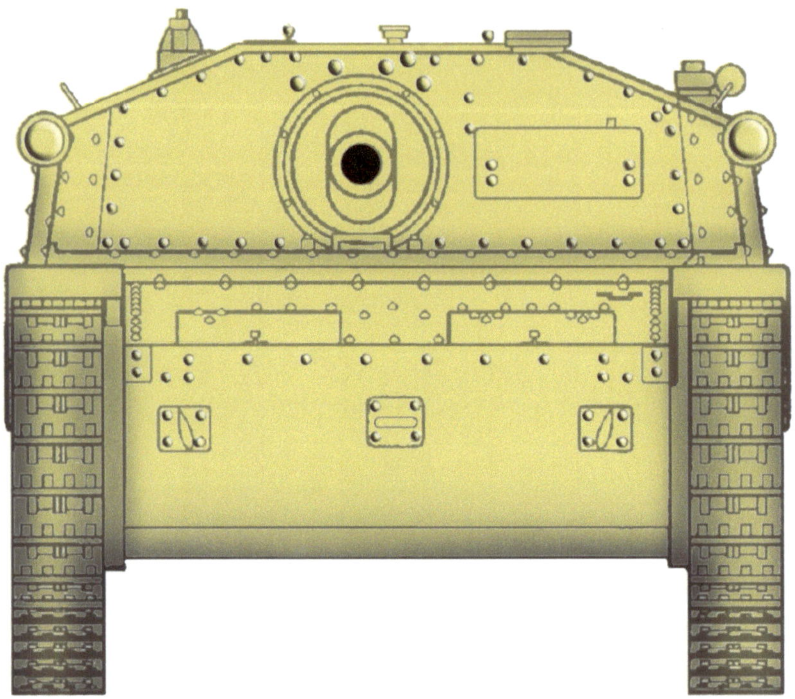

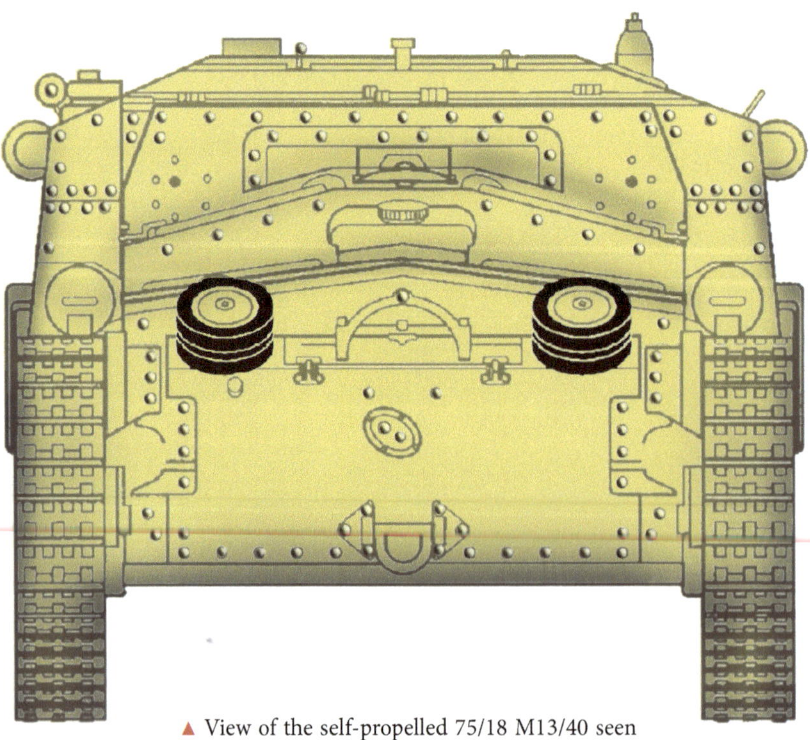

▲ View of the self-propelled 75/18 M13/40 seen from the front and rear.

SELF-PROPELLED 75/34 M15-42 IN ROME, SEPTEMBER 1943

▲ Self-propelled 75-34 M.42 3rd Platoon 2nd Company of the 'Lancers of Vittorio Emanuele II' regiment, part of the Ariete Armoured Division, Rome, September 1943.

▲ An Italian 75/34 self-propelled vehicle that has just been captured by the British soldiers of the 78th Infantry Division who are examining the vehicle. The British have also already erased the German *balkenkreuz* and put the *battleaxe* badge of their division in its place. Italy, May 1944.

CAMOUFLAGE AND DISTINGUISHING MARKS

The background colors of the self-propelled vehicles, both M13-14-15 and 75/34, from their creation until 1945, (the operational period of such use is indicated in brackets) used for all armored vehicles were: gray green R.A. (1936-1945), dark chocolate (1936-1941), reddish brown (1936-1943), ochre (for prototypes), sand (1941-1945), dark sand (1943-1945), dark gray (1941-1943). Medium green (1936-1943) and dark red (for prototypes) were used for camouflage. Medium tanks were not yet in service at the time of the Ethiopian War 1935-1936 and the Spanish Civil War 1937-1939.

National territory 1936-1940 - substantial prevalence of gray green.

Occupation of Albania and French front 1939-1940 - gray green.

Greece and Yugoslavia campaign 1940-1941 - gray green possibly camouflaged with green and sand-colored speckles.

East Africa 1940-1941 - gray green or in old Ethiopian campaign camouflage reddish brown with green speckles.

North Africa 1940-1943 - at first only gray green, the color in which they were generally landed at destination ports, then sand color in the various variegated versions. Not used in the Russian Campaign 1941-1943.

RSI 1943-1945 - green gray, dark sand yellow, reddish brown with medium dense green mottling, in the uniform German panzer grey color. Particularly dark sand-colored were the tanks of the "Leonessa" and to some extent the "Leoncello" and "San Giusto." We also report the presence of elaborate camouflage in irregular checkerboards of sandy yellow background and green and brown patches.

■ SELF-PROPELLED TANKS BADGES

To recognize individual armored vehicles in military operations, even for Italy, it became necessary to introduce an identification system, partly because at least initially there were no tanks with radio equipment installed. In fact, radios began to be installed with some regularity only from 1941. At first, flags with red or white drapes were used to communicate.

The first chart of distinctive tank markings dates from 1925 and was very complex and articulate, to the point of excess. Number groups were not introduced until 1927, after the establishment of the Tank Regiment; new regulations were then issued in 1928. These official charts never mentioned the markings for self-propelled units. It so happened that many units followed its directives, while others did their own thing. Thus the most disparate symbols appeared on the hulls, from the black tortoise of the "Ariete" Division, to the centaur with bow on horseback for the division of the same name. Colorful geometric figures (circles, triangles or rhombuses) of various sizes were used. Soon, however, the use of triangles (typical of only self-propelled vehicles) was standardized, at least in the "Ariete".

These were triangles with the tip pointing downward, and upside down in the case of command tanks. One-color or two-color in the color choices already adopted in tanks: the first battery had red, the 2nd blue, the 3rd yellow, the 4th green; white was reserved for command tanks. The first batteries had only one color triangle. The triangles of the various batteries were surmounted by an Arabic number (of the color of the battery) indicative of the self-propelled unit in the organic formation of the department.

Some self-propelled units adopted colored guidons on the radio antennas, of the same color for each group: for example, the DLIV group had red cloth guidons with a different yellow central geometric design for each of the twelve self-propelled units in the department. Such symbols, for this group belonging to the Littorio Division, were also painted, again in red, on the rear bulkhead of the hull.

The self-propelled vehicles of the CCXXX Assault Group operating in Sicily in 1943, instead of the triangle, used as a badge a kind of black guidon, also triangular in color, with the effigy of a skull resting on white crossbones (see p. 46).

Each vehicle, then, could also be distinguished by a precise designation written in white on a rectangle on a red background placed on the side of the hull, which also served as an identification abbreviation for radio calls. The first battery of the DLVII group, for example, chose the names of the great Italian condottieri of the Renaissance: Fieramosca, Biancamano, Malatesta, Carmagnola, Montecuccoli, Colleoni, and Fortebraccio while the self-propelled guns of the 2nd battery used names of ancient weapons: Arrow, Sling, Strale, Picca, Dardo, and Alabarda.

Other groups adopted the names of old guns and artillery such as: Archibugio, Spingarda, Colubruna, etc. (see pp. 31 and 43).

Several self-propelled units, in honor of the fact that they belonged to the artillery, bore painted the emblem of armored artillery (crossed guns surmounted by grenade and horizontal flame) on the right front side of the casemate (as a rule it was present on the left side). Over time, however, we saw more and more self-propelled units adopt the use of the colored rectangles already in use in medium and light tanks. Self-propelled batteries were represented by rectangles colored in the manner already indicated for triangles.

As an aerial identification mark, a white Savoy cross was sometimes painted on the vehicles, placed, depending on the type of vehicle, on the turret or engine compartment ceiling. Beginning in 1941, a white disk about 70 cm in diameter was painted instead of the cross. Despite circulars and directions as already mentioned, there were numerous exceptions and variations to the official regulations.

The self-propelled vehicles that later passed into the hands of the Italian Social Republic showed painted the distinctive signs of the various regions: the "Leoncello" was depicted by a black lion clutching a fascio littorio looking to the left on a white background. The "Leonessa" had a somewhat more complicated insignia formed by the red M of Mussolini, cut by a black-colored bundle and underneath the always black inscription "GNR."

The "Leoncello" Armored Group used, instead of colored rectangles, a tricolor flag of the same size, with white numbering to indicate the Squadron number (above the tricolor) and the tank number (below).

The "San Giusto" Armored Squadron Group adopted a symbol consisting of a simple tricolor, on which the outline of a black tank was added starting in the spring of 1944. The tricolor was later (fall 1944) replaced with a waving one and the silhouette of the tank with that of a self-propelled vehicle. The self-propelled vehicles captured and later reused by the Germans, (and in addition to these also the new ones ordered after the armistice of 194) bore the typical German army markings starting with the black and white ritterkreuz in its various fashions. The same was true of the camouflage, with "German" colors for the vehicles that had become part of the Germanic army.

▲ Self-propelled 75/18 M.41 Tank 'Colubrina' of the DLVII Assault Group in Sicily, Italy, August 1943.
Like the tank of the 'Piscitelli' Group, this too had received an archaic designation.

▲▼ M13/40 tanks with their crews on the outside of the vehicle. Libyan front, 1940-1941.

SELF-PROPELLED 75/18 M14-41, ITALY 1943

▲ Self-propelled 75/18 M.41 of the Littorio Armoured Division in Sicily, Italy, August 1943.

SELF-PROPELLED 75/18 M14-41 SICILY, ITALY 1943

▲ Self-propelled 75/18 M.41 belonging to the CCXXX Assault Group operating in Sicily, Italy 1943.
This group had adopted a symbol that differentiated it from the others: a black pennant with skull and crossbones.

PRODUCTION AND EXPORT

About 288 self-propelled vehicles were built since the start of the war, based on the hulls of 60 M13/40s, 162 M14/41 tanks (including self-propelled and command) and another 66 M 15/42s. The number of total vehicles in the different variants, however, is not certain, since the Germans produced their own, and the numberings, mainly for the M41 model, are quite different according to sources. Since production began in wartime, there were no international markets available to which the vehicles could be disposed of, as was the case with light tanks, for example. The tanks, mainly due to wartime events, ended up in the hands of different belligerent and/or allied and former allied nations.

- Royal Army: purchaser and major user of much of the production of medium armored vehicles.
- Australia: as a result of the battles in the North African desert, Australian troops took possession of a number of armored vehicles, mainly medium tanks, but probably also self-propelled vehicles, which were restored by the Australians themselves and repainted with typical colors and distinctive markings (the famous white kangaroos).
- Great Britain: as above, British troops also got their hands on some Italian medium tanks.
- Italian Social Republic: after the collapse of Italy following the events of September 8, a new state was created in German-controlled northern Italy. The RSI used all the military means of the Royal Army already at its disposal.
- German Army: similarly, and in a massive and selective manner, the German Army, after September 8 also confiscated and repurposed all Italian assets at its disposal. In some cases even reactivating production assembly lines (especially in the case of M15 vehicles and derived self-propelled vehicles).

MAIN USER

Medium tanks were used by the armies indicated above, but obviously its main user was Italy and its armored units: by the Royal Army above all but also, after the Armistice, by the National Republican Army and the National Republican Guard, following the establishment of the Italian Social Republic in 1943. A few vehicles, finally, were also captured in European theaters of war, particularly in Dalmatia and the Balkans, and captured and reused by Yugoslav partisans and again by the Greek resistance. Some of these vehicles remained in service in Italy for a short time longer during the immediate postwar years.

▲ The crew of an Italian self-propelled vehicle observes the photographer filming them as they pass under the Cestia pyramid in Rome in the September days when Italian troops tried to block the German occupation of the capital.

▼ A self-propelled vehicle knocked out in the clashes in Rome in September 1942 (Wikipedia).

ITALIAN SELF-PROPELLED 75-18 AND 75-34

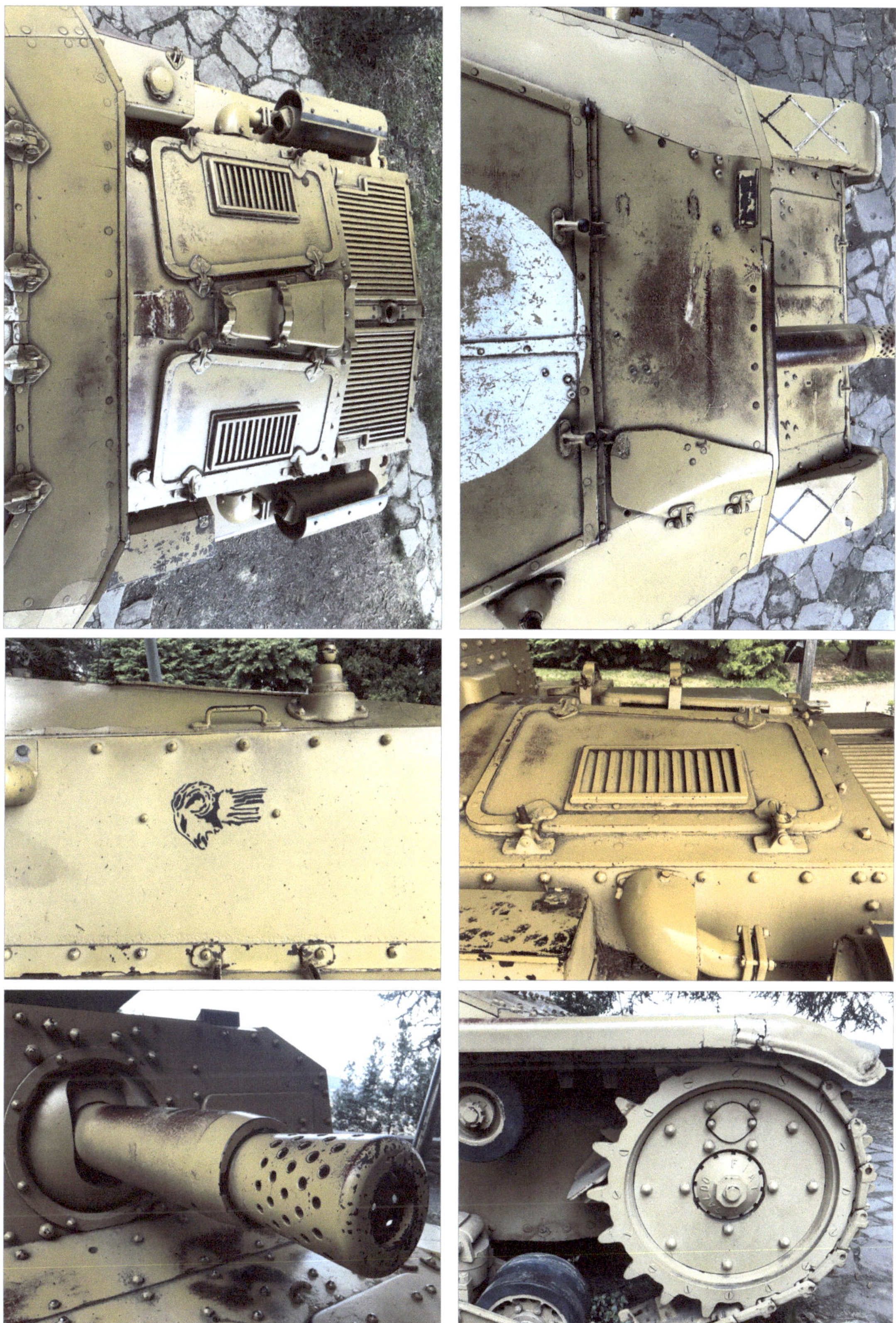

▲ Details of the self-propelled 75/18 M.42 preserved at the Parco della Rocca in Bergamo. Photo by the author.

▲ Rear of the self-propelled 75/18 (note the soldier hiding in a hole) (Wikipedia).

▼ British soldiers intent on examining a series of German and Italian armoured vehicles (the two self-propelled vehicles in the background) Italy, 2 June 1944. Wikipedia - Author's colouring.

ITALIAN SELF-PROPELLED 75-18 AND 75-34

SELF-PROPELLED 75/18 M.42 GERMAN VERSION, ITALY 1944

▲ Self-propelled 75/18 M.42 Panzerjager Abt. 278th Infantry Division, Ancona, Italy 1944.

	75/18 M13/40	75/18 M14/41	75/18/34 M15/42
Length	4915 mm	4915 mm	5060 mm
Width	2200 mm	2200 mm	2280 mm
Height	1850 mm	1850 mm	2370 mm
Minimum bottom-hull height from the ground	0,38 m	0,38 m	0,41 m
Weight in combat order	13.100 kg	13.500 kg	15.000 kg
Crew	4	4	4
Engine	M 13: Fiat-SPA 8T M.40 diesel 8-cylinder V-shaped engine, 11.140 cm³ M 14: Fiat SPA 15T M.41 diesel 8-cylinder V-shaped engine, 11.980 cm³ M 15: FIAT-SPA 15TB M.42 8-cylinder V-shaped, gasoline-powered		
Maximum speed	31,8 km/h on road 13 km/h off road	35 km/h on road 13 km/h off road	39 km/h on road 14 km/h off road
Range	215 km on road 5 h off road	210 km on road 5 h off road	200 km on road 5 h off road
Tank capacity	180 L	180 L	307 L
Armor thickness	From 6 to 50 mm	From 6 to 50 mm	From 6 to 55 mm
Armament	1 75/18 Mod. 1934 howitzer with 44 rounds. 1 Breda Mod. 30 6.5-mm machine gun.	1 75/18 Mod. 1934 howitzer with 44 rounds. 1 Breda Mod. 38 8-mm machine gun.	1 75/18 howitzer and then one 75/34 howitzer. 1 Breda Mod. 38 8-mm machine gun.

▼ Self-propelled 75718 M.41 in the Fossati-Ansaldo factories. State Archives. (Author's colouring).

SELF-PROPELLED 75/34 M15-42, ITALY 1943

▲ Self-propelled 75-34 M.42 Italian unknown unit, operating in the area of the Latium lakes, Italy, summer 1943.

▲▼ Towards the end of the war, some RSI and even German vehicles ended up in the hands of the partisan forces who, in the euphoria of a terrible war that was drawing to a close, painted their mottos and insignia, as in the case of these self-propelled vehicles and light tanks on 'parade' in Turin. (Archive Paolo Crippa).

SELF-PROPELLED 75/34 M15-42, RSI 1943-1945

▲ Self-propelled 75-34 M.42 of the 'San Giusto' Armoured Group, R.S.I, Italy 1943-1945.

SELF-PROPELLED 75/34 M15-42 GERMAN VERSION, BALKANS 1944

▲ Self-propelled 75-34 M.42 in the German Army in the Balkans, 1944.

SELF-PROPELLED 75/34 M15-42 GERMAN VERSION, ITALY 1944

▲ Self-propelled 75-34 M.42 in force of the German army on the Gothic line 171st Panzer Divison, Italy, May 1944.

BIBLIOGRAPHY

- *Semovente da 75/18 : tecnica e storia del primo semovente italiano.* Pignato, Nicola (2010). Parma: Albertelli.
- *Semoventi M41 & M42.* Daniele Guglielmi. Armor Photogallery -Broncos (in inglese)
- *Veicoli da Combattimento dell'Esercito Italiano dal 1939 al 1945.* Falessi, Cesare; Pafi, Benedetto (1976). Intyrama books.
- *Tank Power vol. CLXXXIII 443. Semovente da 75/32-34-46, 90/53, 105/25* - Janusz Ledwoch Polonia Widawnictwo militaria.
- *Semovente da 75/18. Tank Power vol. CXII 365* - Janusz Ledwoch. Polonia Widawnictwo militaria.
- *Mussolini Tanks - Tank Powwer vol. XXIX.* Polonia Widawnictwo militaria.
- *Italian Medium tank M13/40, M14/41 & M15/42* - Luca Stefano Cristni colla TEW Soldiershop. Italia 2022.
- *Semoventi da 47/32, 90/53 e 75/18 in Sicilia.* Ediz. illustrata - Lorenzo Bovi, Antonio e Andrea Talillo. Ardite edizioni 2021, Italia.
- *Italian Armored Vehicles of World War Two.* Pignato, Nicola (2004).Squadron/Signal publications.
- *Storia dei mezzi corazzati.* Pignato, Nicola. Vol. II. Fratelli Fabbri Editori.
- *I reparti corazzati italiani nei Balcani,* Paolo Crippa e Carlo Cucut. Soldiershop 2019.
- *I reparti corazzati del R.E. E l'armistizio 1° Volume,* Paolo Crippa. Soldiershop 2021.
- *I reparti corazzati del R.E. E l'armistizio 2° Volume,* Paolo Crippa. Soldiershop 2021.
- *Il gruppo corazzato del Leoncello,* Paolo Crippa. Soldiershop 2021.
- *I mezzi blindo-corazzati italiani 1923-1943,* Nicola Pignato, Storia Militare, 2005.
- *Gli autoveicoli da combattimento dell'Esercito Italiano, Volume secondo (1940-1945),* Stato Maggiore dell'Esercito, Ufficio Storico, Nicola Pignato e Filippo Cappellano, 2002.
- *Corazzati Italiani 1939-1945,* Nico Sgarlato, War Set n°10, 2006.
- *Mezzi dell'Esercito Italiano 1935-45,* Ugo Barlozzetti & Alberto Pirella, Editoriale Olimpia, 1986.
- *Corazzati e blindati italiani dalle origini allo scoppio della seconda guerra mondiale,* David Vannucci, Editrice Innocenti, 2003.
- *"L'Ariete a Bir-El Gobi". Storia Militare (in Italian).* Maraziti, Antonio (Gennaio 2005). Albertelli edizioni.
- *Il gruppo corazzato "San Giusto" dal Regio Esercito alla RSI 1934-1945,* Stefano Di Giusto, Laran Éditions, 2008.
- *I reparti corazzati della Repubblica Sociale Italiana 1943/1945,* Paolo Crippa, Marvia Edizioni, 2006.
- *Storia dell'Ansaldo 6. Dall'IRI alla guerra 1930-1945,* Gabriele De Rosa, Gius. Laterza & Figli, 1999.
- *Military vehicle prints series nr. 37.* Nicola Pignato, Bellona Polonia.

TITLES PUBLISHED OR IN WORKING

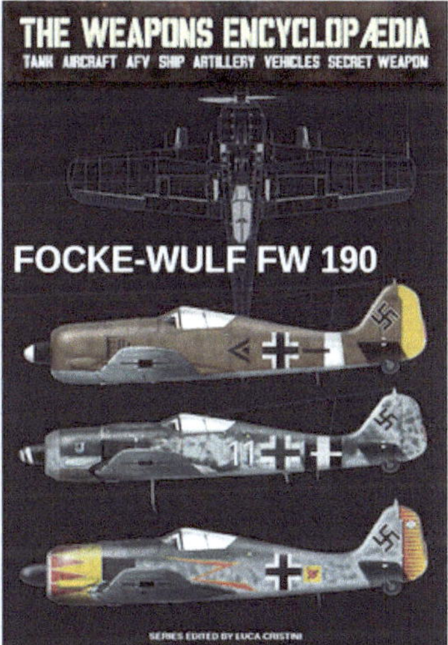

TWE-003 EN

www.ingramcontent.com/pod-product-compliance
Lightning Source LLC
LaVergne TN
LVHW071621180726
843512LV00002B/216